797.1
Nab   Nabhan, Marty
     White water rafting

White Water Rafting

by Marty Nabhan

**Published By
Capstone Press, Inc.
Mankato, Minnesota USA**

Distributed By

CHILDRENS PRESS®

CHICAGO

CIP
LIBRARY OF CONGRESS CATALOGING IN PUBLICATION DATA

Nabhan, Martin.
   White water rafting / by Martin Nabhan.
      p. cm. – (Action sports)
   Summary: Describes the history, equipment, and techniques of white water rafting.

   ISBN 1-56065-053-2:
   1. Rafting (Sports) – Juvenile literature.
   (1. Rafting (Sports).) I. Title. II. Series.
   GV780-N33   1989
   797.1'22 – dc20   89-27874
                                                        CIP
                                                         AC

PHOTO CREDITS

Jeff Behan: 3, 29, 31, 34, 45, 48
Marshall-McKee: 15, 19, 23, 25
Whitewater Voyages: 6, 4, 40
Wildwater Expeditions: 10, 37, 43

CAPSTONE PRESS
Box 669, Mankato, MN 56001

Contents

A Run Through White Water 5

How Rafting Became a Sport 11

Clothing, Equipment and
    Tips for Safe Rafting 14

Different Types of Rivers 21

Canoes, Kayaks, Inner Tubes
    and Other Floaters 28

Camping Out on an
    Overnight River Trip 33

Fun and Danger in the Rapids 38

How to Get Ready for
    Your Own River Run 42

Glossary 46

A Run Through White Water

The hot morning sun warms your bright orange life jacket. Sweat runs down your forehead. You smell the air, thick with the scent of pine trees. Meanwhile, gray rubber rafts bob at the edge of the river, waiting for their passengers.

The river guide ends his safety talk. It's time!

You quickly grab a plastic **paddle** for rowing. "Over here!" your friends say, and you join them at one of the rafts. Together you push the raft into the river. The ice cold water seeps into your old tennis shoes. You jump into the bobbing raft as the guide pushes it further out in the river.

The bottom of the raft is thin. You can feel it bounce over small rocks until the water gets deeper. You sit on the edge of the raft itself, holding on tight with your feet. Your guide hops in and you're off, gliding over the babbling water.

"I forgot to tell you," your guide smiles. "You will be getting wet."

Freezing water suddenly crashes against your back. The first water fight has started. Another raft comes close from behind. Their guide, armed with his **bailing bucket,** takes aim and throws more water. You and your friends dig your paddles into the river and splash water back at the attacking raft. Luckily, the wind is in your favor. The other raft gives up and calls you the winner.

Your clothes are soaked, but the cool water feels good in the baking sun. The tall, green pines come nearly to the river bank. A deer near the edge laps up some water. It stops and gazes cautiously as your raft floats by. The guide points to an eagle perched up in a tree, looking for fish in the clear water. You never thought nature could be so beautiful.

You paddle with the rest of the crew. The guide barks commands like a slave ship captain. Soon, your crew is able to steer the raft just by paddling.

"Good," the guide says. "Teamwork is important on the river."

You relax. Sitting on the edge, you dangle one foot in the rippling water. A breeze blows over the river, giving you a chill from your wet clothes. With your expert guide you feel safe and calm, as though you were on a ride at Disneyland.

A roar rises in the distance like a hundred lions calling for their dinner. You look ahead but see nothing. The guide grips his paddle tightly and keeps watch up front. You can tell the time for goofing around is over. Everyone is tense, waiting for orders from the guide. The guide is quiet and peers forward. The river bends gently, and then you see it: **white water!** Large boulders sprout through the bubbling waves.

The guide spots the best path through the **rapids**. "Keep to the center!" he yells, as the river roar gets louder. The water gets faster, and you see it rush through two rocks ahead. "Forward!" shouts the guide.

The crew paddles hard, listening to the guide's every word. Your heart beats rapidly. Though there is water everywhere, your mouth goes dry. For the first time on the trip, you are truly nervous. There is no time to be scared, though. You pay close attention to the guide. This is not the time for a mistake.

"Paddle harder." You fight to keep the raft pointing straight ahead. If it turns sideways, it might flip over in the rough water.

The raft goes over the first bump, and the crew is hit with a spray of water. The two rocks are closer, and the guide steers to the center. The force of the water grabs the raft and pulls it between the rocks. You hang on and dig your feet tighter into the raft. The raft slides down like a roller coaster. It hits a wall of water and springs upward, dousing everyone on board.

The crew stops paddling, stunned by the splash of water. "Forward!" the guide shouts. "Do not stop now." Without thinking, the crew starts paddling again. You see your raft start to turn as it raises above the next wave. You paddle with all your might.

The raft bursts over the top of the wave and plunges down again into the white water. This time the crew remembers to keep paddling forward. Soon the water becomes smooth, and the roar is behind you.

You and your friends laugh. Your nerves go back to normal, and your heart slows back down. You have passed through your first rapids.

"Turn around," the guide says. You smile as you

see the faces of the people on the other raft. They look terrified as they shoot through the white water.

How Rafting Became A Sport

People have been riding rivers for years. When man learned that wood could float, he tied trees together to make rafts or carved canoes out of large logs. The difference back then was that no one rode rivers just for fun.

Humans found that the best way to get from one place to another was on the water. Rivers were like highways. It was easier to put goods on a boat than to carry them over the rough land. Native American Indians used hollow logs, or "dugouts," as **canoes**.

Then the white men came. Many of them were looking for a way to get across North America by boat, using the rivers. They called their idea the Northwest Passage. They hoped it would be a new way to get to the Pacific Ocean and on to China. In 1534, the French explorer Cartier went up the St. Lawrence River as far as he could.

One of the most famous trips to find the Northwest Passage was taken in 1804 by Lewis and Clark. They and their men rode many rivers for three years. It was far from fun! Their big boats were no match for white water. When they got near rapids, they pulled their boats out of the water. Then they carried the boats and all their goods, sometimes for many miles. When the river was calm again, they put their boats back in. They found out there was no Northwest Passage.

Other men came for the fur trade. They traveled out west to hunt beavers and sell their furs. On the Mississippi River, men used large wooden rafts to get around.

In 1869, Major John Wesley Powell came west with nine men to explore the Green and Colorado Rivers. They found many beautiful canyons. Red and orange cliffs rose from the ground like towers. The water was brown with mud. It looked like a river of chocolate milk. In the Grand Canyon they crossed huge rapids. Even though one of their boats broke into pieces, they finished their great journey.

News of their trip made others excited to explore other rivers. Nathaniel Galloway was one such man, and in 1896 he tried something new. To "row" a boat you push with your legs and pull back on the oars. The problem with this is that in white water you would have your back to the rapids. You cannot see where you are going! Nat Galloway solved the problem. He turned his boat around and rowed against the water. Of course, the rivers were stronger and pushed him along. The backward rowing, though, slowed him down. He could see the rapids and safely guide his boat through them.

In 1945, after World War II, army stores started selling left-over rubber life rafts. Thousands of people who would not have thought of riding rivers bought these rafts and tried floating down local rapids. Still, the biggest rivers were too dangerous to ride.

In the early 1950s, Georgie White and her friend Harry Aleson visited the Grand Canyon. They watched the rough Colorado River surging along. This was the same river that tore one of Major Powell's boats to pieces. Georgie and Harry were great swimmers, and dove in with no boat. They just had on their life jackets. The raging river tossed them back and forth. They disappeared from sight. Their friends thought they had died. Tired and worn out, Georgie and Harry came out of the river many miles downstream. "I do not want to see another river," Harry said.

But Georgie loved the river. She wanted other people to have as much fun there as she did. One day in 1954 she watched a leaf bob up and down on the river next to a toy boat. Georgie had an idea. She tied three rubber rafts together and sent them down the river. People said it would never work, but Georgie proved them wrong. Her three rafts crept down the great rapids without ever turning over. She had found a safe way people could ride the Colorado River in the Grand Canyon. Her rafts, called **G-rigs**, are still popular today.

White-water rafting has become a big sport. Rafts can move and bend with the rapids. They are good for beginners because they are safe. Rafting skills are not hard to learn. Thrills are there for newcomers. Young people, the blind, those who can't walk, all can have a white-water experience on rafts.

There is just one important rule: think safety.

Clothing, Equipment and Tips for Safe Rafting

A raft crawls over the waves. It shapes itself to the water. That is why the ride is so smooth. Do

not be fooled, though. The river can still be dangerous.

A river often starts high up in the mountains. It may start as a spring rushing forth from the ground. Snow in the mountains melts. The melted snow flows into streams. This water, like all water, follows the law of gravity. It will continue to flow until it reaches its lowest point. As the amount of water gets bigger, the course it follows becomes a river.

The path that a river follows is always changing. Sometimes it is wide and deep. Other times it can be narrow and shallow. Sometimes the path slopes gently. Other times it can drop off quickly.

Have you ever been on a freeway or road that narrows? There is still the same number of cars, but the space they have to get through is less. The cars have to slow down to get through. If they didn't slow down, they would run into each other and crash everywhere.

Water cannot slow down. It is not afraid to crash into itself. As a river's path gets more shallow or narrow, the same amount of water still needs to get through. The water running into itself or into rocks makes the rumbling waves and roaring sound that we call "white water."

If you are not careful, there are four things on a river trip that can give you trouble: the water, the wind, the rocks and the sun. Let us look at some of the equipment you need to insure a safe white-water trip.

A good raft is your best protection in the water. A raft should be sturdy, built with white-water in mind. Many rafts sold in stores are fine for lakes and calm streams, but would be torn apart in real rapids. The best rafts are made of nylon, Hypalon or other tough, flexible material. The raft protects you from the rocks the same way the tires of your bike protect you from stones on the road.

There are two main types of rafts: oar rafts and paddle rafts. With oar rafts, all the work is done by the guide. A wood or aluminum frame is tied on the raft, with **oarlocks** to hold the oars in place. The oars can be made of aluminum or hard wood. The frame should be secured so no sharp corners puncture the raft or the passengers! The guide mans both oars, and is in charge of steering and movement. The passengers can sit back, relax, and enjoy the ride.

In paddle rafts, each person on board is part of the paddling team. They have an active part in getting the raft in position, under the guide's orders. The paddles are made of aluminum or strong plastic. They float, too, so if you drop one in the water you will hopefully see it again. It is always a good idea to carry spare paddles along with you.

Rope should also be on board. Rope along the sides is good for holding on through rough water. It can be used for tying the raft, and for rescues as well. Any extra rope should be coiled and stored so you do not get tangled in it.

An air pump and patch kit will come in handy in case of a raft puncture. It is always best to be prepared. A first aid kit is also needed. Each raft should have its own bail bucket. These buckets are used for scooping water out of the raft. (They are helpful in water fights, too.)

What you wear on the trip is also very important. Every member of the crew must wear a **life jacket** at all times. A life jacket can keep you afloat if you fall out of the raft. The jacket should fit snugly. It will not do you much good if the jacket floats but you slip out of it.

River water is often very cold. The wind can be even more chilling. Because of this, a danger on the river is **hypothermia**. Hypothermia is a big word that simply means your body has gotten too cold. If you get hypothermia, your body shivers and shakes, trying to keep warm. Hypothermia slows down your heart and can cause death.

The right clothes can help to prevent hypothermia. Clothes made of wool and synthetics are the best. They can keep you warm, even when they get wet. Avoid clothes made of cotton. They dry slowly and stay cold when wet. If the wind is chilly, you may need to wear rubber rain jackets and rain pants. Rubber rain clothes are often big and bulky, but you will be glad you have them if an icy wind blows across the river. It is a good idea to take a dry change of clothes along, especially if you are camping overnight. Keep them in a plastic bag or other container so they can stay dry while you are on the river.

Shoes are also a must, but not to keep your feet warm. If you fall out of the boat, you should keep your feet in front of you to shield against boulders. Walking to and from the boat across sharp rocks might cut your bare feet. Old tennis shoes are the best. They will also keep you from slipping on smooth rocks and falling into the water.

Waterproof bags or cans are good things to have with you. You can store food, cameras, spare clothes, and anything else you want to keep dry. And be sure to bring insect repellant.

Some experts who go on the most challenging rivers wear helmets. These give them protection against hitting their heads on rocks.

"If I could do it all over again," said Aline Cannon, a California white-water rafter, after running the Kern River, "I would take sun screen." You do not often think of the sun as an enemy, but too much time in it can damage your skin. Your clothes should cover as much of your body as possible. You can rub sun screen on your skin for more help. The lotion can wash off, so repeat it often.

Taking along the right equipment and clothing can make your trip safer and more fun. Your best protection, however, will be what you know about the river.

Different Types of Rivers

One of the first things you will notice on the river is the beauty of nature. Riding rivers gives you a chance to see the country in a way that few people do.

Rivers come in all sizes and shapes. Some are in lush green mountains, with trees on both sides. Some wander through valleys and across the prairie grass. Some wind through deserts and cut their path deep into huge canyons.

Some rivers are warm; others are cold. Some rivers are flat; others are steep. Some rivers creep by slowly; others race like the wind. Some rivers are crystal clear; others are as brown as mud. Some rivers are perfect for beginners. Others are for experts only.

Because rivers are so different, learn about your river before you go. Are there a lot of rapids? Is there overnight camping? What is the history of the river? Are there many mosquitoes? What will the weather be like when you plan on going?

A bike rider learns the traffic laws and knows how to read the signs: stop, go, right turn only, one way. Like a street sign, a river can also be read. The river guide must know how to read a river. It is a good idea for all crew members to have that skill as well. Here are some signs and clues to reading a river.

You hear white water before you see it. When you hear white water getting closer, get ready to follow the orders of your guide.

When the rapids come into view, you may see paths of smooth water that head into them. They look like Vs pointing into the white water. They are caused by water rushing through two obstacles. These Vs, called **tongues** or **chutes**, usually mark the best way into the rapids. If there

are many of them, follow the biggest one. That is where most of the water is going. They are often the deepest part of that white water.

Standing waves are just what the name says. These waves stay in one place. They are caused by water rushing over a shallow area and splashing down on calm water. Because they form a mound of water, they are often called "haystacks." A good guide will know if the standing waves are safe. If they are safe, the best way to go is over them. Your ride will be like sitting on a bucking bronco at the rodeo.

Eddies are calm areas in the water just past obstacles. After running a rapid, your guide may want to paddle to an eddy to rest.

Reversals are some of the most dangerous forms on the river. They have many names. They may be called "souse holes," "backrollers," or "keepers." When water is moving quickly and hits slower water, it can rush back against itself. These reversals can be found past boulders or at the bottom of falls. Even standing waves can turn into reversals. They are dangerous because they can keep your raft caught in one spot. The water keeps rushing under the raft while the reversal keeps pushing it back. Some objects stay in reversals for days. Your raft may take on (fill up with) water. The raft may even flip. If the

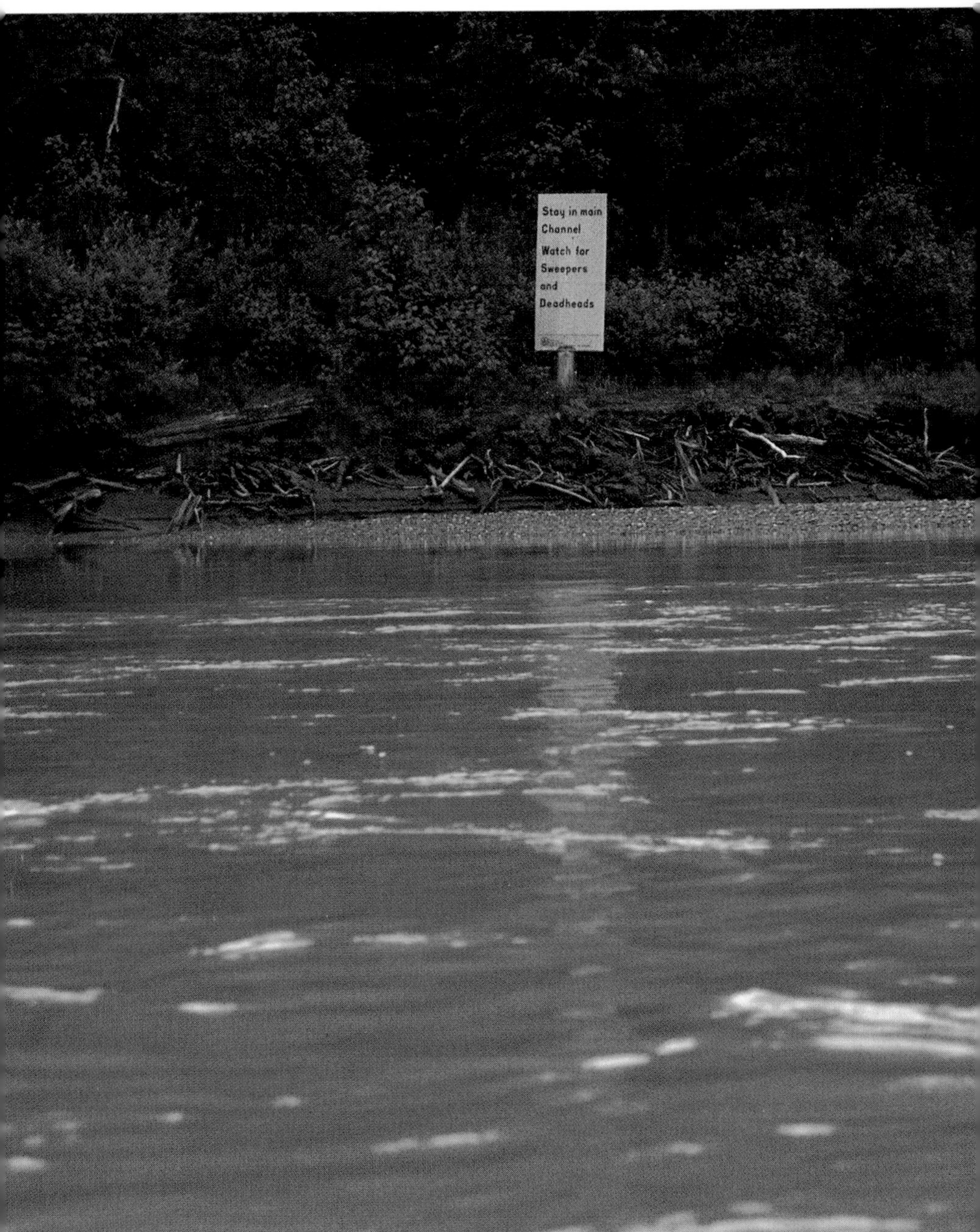
Stay in main
Channel
Watch for
Sweepers
and
Deadheads

raft flips, you could get caught in the reversal yourself. The best advice for reversals is to stay clear.

Shallows occur when the river widens. There are a lot of rocks in shallows. The guide needs to keep his eyes open to pick his way through.

Bends in the river are sometimes called **dog-legs** because of their shape. The water is fastest on the outside of bends. It is best to stay on the inside. Trees and other obstacles, called **strainers**, are sometimes on the outside of bends. Some river guides consider these the most dangerous of all obstacles. Water rushes quickly through strainers. Rafts and people, though, cannot get through. The raft could flip, or you could get stuck under the rushing water. Stay away from strainers. Finally, stay away from steep falls and holes.

As you can see, some obstacles are tougher than others. Some people seek tough challenges. Others would rather have calm waters. How can you know which river you are choosing?

Because rivers are so different, they are rated. Experts get together and look at the rapids. They call the easiest ones Class I, and the hardest Class VI. This is a guide to the ratings:

Class I Very Easy. There are few bumps and

ripples on these rivers. Waves are small, and there are few or no obstacles. These are good rivers for beginners to learn on.

Class II Easy. The current is a little faster than Class I. Waves are up to a foot high. Some obstacles are here but they are easy to paddle through.

Class III Medium. Here is where the real white water starts. These rivers have numerous waves, up to three feet high. The rapids still have clear passages, but are not suggested for beginners. Hang on to your seats!

Class IV Difficult. This river will have long and hard rapids. Scouting is recommended for the raft guides. Many obstructions are here. The waves are strong and irregular.

Class V Very difficult. For experts only, these rivers have big drops, huge waves, lots of obstacles, and violent current. Scouting the river is necessary before trying the rapids. Helmets may be necessary.

Class VI Unnavigable. That means do not try it. These rivers are nearly impossible to run. They are dangerous, and life threatening. Even for experts, these rivers are a risk to life.

Just because a river is rated low does not

mean it is safe. A Class I river can turn into a Class II after a heavy rain. In the early spring, mountain snow melts, and the large runoff can change a river's class. Also, some people may rate a river differently than others.

A good thing to remember is that rivers are always changing. They change from year to year. They even change from hour to hour. That is what makes white-water rafting so exciting. There are always new challenges on the rapids.

Canoes, Kayaks, Inner Tubes and other Floaters

The noon sun rises high, drying your wet clothes. You look forward to the next water fight. The river is calm now. The guide says it would be a good time to hop in the water and float for a while, using only your life jacket.

You hang both feet into the water, checking the temperature. It is very cold and you think it best to go in a little at a time. A slight shove at your back changes your mind. A friend pushes you in, and you splash under the cool, clear

liquid. Your life jacket pushes you back up quickly. Others join you, and soon the river is dotted by swimmers in life jackets.

You gently float down the river facing forward. You keep your feet in front of you in case you come up against any rocks. It is better to push off rocks with your tennis shoes than your knees or elbows.

You stay close to the raft. If the guide calls, you want to be ready to climb back in.

You feel small against the great river. Mountains rise up on your right. You see some of your friends splashing each other. You notice your group is not alone on the river. Other crafts paddle nearby.

A man in a red kayak waves to you as he darts between rocks. A **kayak** is a long craft shaped like a cigar. The rider sits with his legs inside it, his body poking out through the top. You need a lot of skill to ride a kayak through white water. Kayaks are designed to make sharp turns and get through small openings. Every stroke of the paddle counts. Kayaks often turn upside down in white water, but they do not sink. The man plugs the kayak like a cork in a bottle. His helmet keeps his head from hitting rocks. One of the first strokes a kayaker learns is the "**eskimo roll.**" When his kayak turns over, one powerful thrust of his paddle rolls him right side up.

Two men pass by in their aluminum canoe. Canoes are long and thin and bend up at both ends. Like all people on the river, these men also have on life jackets.

Many inflatables became popular in the late 1970s. Today you may see inflatable kayaks and other crafts on the river.

Inner tubes are popular too, but are not good for white water. Taken from old car tires, inner tubes look like giant black Cheerios.

Rafts also come in many sizes. They range from huge **pontoons** to one-man rafts. Some rafts on bigger rivers look like a bunch of sausages tied together. Sometimes guides will put rafts on top of each other and float down the river. Imagine a triple-decker raft!

The guide spots a flat beach on the river bank and calls all hands back on deck. You paddle over to the beach and pull the raft up on dry ground. Some of the rocks near the shore are sharp, and you are glad you wore shoes. The guide ties the bow line of the raft to a tree. He does not want a wave to take the raft away and leave you all stranded on the beach.

On dry ground now, you can take off your life jacket. The cool breeze feels good against your skin. Some of the crew lie on the raft in the sun to work on their tans. Your nose feels a little burnt, so you put on more sun screen.

After a lunch of sandwiches and soft drinks, you are ready for more action. Your guide takes you on a short hike into the forest. When you get back, you cannot resist temptation when you see the friend who pushed you in the water sleeping calmly on the raft. You load the bailing bucket up with water and give him an ice cold surprise!

Camping Out on an Overnight River Trip

Nothing is quite so tiring as a full day of white-water and paddling on a river. The heat, the cold, the exercise, and the water have all teamed up to sap your strength. The sun begins to lower behind the mountains. All the rafts in your group pull off the river to a campsite. Everyone is hungry and tired. You are ready for a good night's rest.

You change into your warm, dry clothes. The campfire is burning bright. As the sun goes down, white dots of light appear in the darkening sky. You set up your mat and sleeping bag before it gets too dark.

Camping on a river trip is like any other camping. You should know what to expect in that area. What animals might you see? Are there any poisonous plants? Does your campsite have a fire permit? Are there restrooms or outhouses? You need to ask these questions and remember some general rules.

Because you are next to the river, there will probably be mosquitoes. Make sure you have a good insect repellant. Beware of ants, bees and wasps, especially if you are allergic to insect bites. They are attracted to sweet smells, so do not wear perfume or hairspray.

You should take care in the wild. Never put your fingers or hands in holes. Turn over rocks and boards very carefully. You may disturb a snake or other creature that wants to be alone. Always watch where you walk.

A good rule is to keep your skin covered. If you walk through grassy areas, tuck your pants into your socks. This keeps ticks from biting into your legs.

Know what poison oak, ivy and sumac look like. You will not have much fun the next day if you are itching from these poisonous plants.

Camping can be some of the most fun you have on your trip. The night sky is beautiful. You can see more stars than you can in the city. You almost think it is not the same sky!

Your guide has brought good food, and you are plenty hungry. You dig into your sizzling steak. The potatoes bake in the crackling fire. After the meal you sit around the fire. Everyone shares stories, songs, jokes, and laughs. You talk about your first day on the river.

You curl into your sleeping bag and rest your tired bones. You hear the river rumbling past. You take one last look at the glowing night sky. You take one last breath of the cool fresh air. Almost instantly, you are asleep.

Your eyes open at the crack of dawn. The sun is not yet up in the morning sky. Bacon and eggs crackle in the skillet. You have a glass of fresh orange juice, wide awake for the new day. You devour breakfast. You know it will be your last meal until after the rapids.

The guide reminds everyone to shake out their clothes, shoes and socks before putting them on. During the night, spiders, scorpions or other creatures might have made a home in them. They may mistake your toes for breakfast.

The guide leads the group back out onto the roaring river. You know that the biggest rapids have been saved for last.

Fun and Danger in the Rapids

"You hear the roar of the rapids, and your heart goes eighty miles an hour," says Julia Phillips of her first river run. "The next thing you know you are in it and you cannot wait to do it again. It is just that exciting."

All types of people ride rivers. Some go for the view of nature. Others enjoy the water. But for most, the main attraction is the thrill of white-water. Even though a raft is the safest way to shoot the rapids, there is always a sense of danger.

"The rapids have names," says Chantel Cannon of Cypress, California. "Some had no names and we got to make up our own."

The names of the rapids seem to warn the visitors. They have names like Disaster Rapid, Death Rock Rapid, Heaven Help You Rapid, Old Scary Rapid, and Meatgrinder.

It is not always fun and games. Sometimes rides on the river get serious.

"We were in a narrow canyon," remembers Bill Webb of his first river trip as a scout. "One of the rafts got wedged on a rock. Water poured into the raft. The guide pulled the boys out onto the rock. The raft began to bend under the water. He was able to pry it free. The force of the river pushed the raft into the clear, but the boys were left on the rock with no way down. Luckily, another raft was right behind, and took the boys to safety."

Rafting is a team sport. Helping each other is the main rule of the river. Beginners especially should go in groups. Accidents do happen. One common danger is when someone is jolted from the raft. The guide must be told quickly of the man overboard.

A river's current is too strong to fight. A person overboard should face down river and keep his feet in front of him. He can paddle with his hands to steer. The life jacket will keep him afloat. The raft will catch up beside him. The man over-

board must stay clear of the raft. The worst thing that could happen is if the raft pinned him against a rock.

Finally, the time you have waited for has arrived. You look ahead and see the last set of rapids on your trip. These are the big ones. "Forward!" commands the guide. Your crew is now well-trained. You work as one, paddling to the best spot to enter the rapids.

The standing waves boil in haystacks. They rise high above your head. The raft enters the tongue and crashes into the wall of water. The wave covers the laughing crew members, but they keep paddling.

Your raft leaps over another wave, and then another. You are surrounded by white water. Some crew members scream as you crash into one more haystack. A final wave of water flies across the raft. Then the water calms.

The guide smiles. He congratulates you on having finished your trip through white-water. You and the crew raise your paddles high in the air. Your cries of delight echo through the canyon.

A question was asked of a group that had just come back from running a river: "If you had it to do all over again, would you do anything differently?"

Kylie Sorensen seemed to sum it up for everybody. "I would stay longer," she said.

How to Get Ready for Your Own River Run

White-water rafting is not for everyone. But it can be for you! Running the rapids is for both young and old people. One woman started rafting when she was 70 years old. Boys and girls can start learning by the age of eight. You do not need to be strong or big to ride a river. You just need the desire. Do you want to go white-water rafting? Here's how you can get started.

First, you should like the water. Do you enjoy other water sports? Have you been in boats before? One thing is sure with white-water rafting: you will get wet.

Second, you should like swimming. If you do not know how to swim, learn. If you are just learning, practice to get better. There is always room to improve. You do not have to be an

Olympic champion swimmer to ride rapids. If you are a good swimmer, you will be more confident in the water.

Third, you should like nature. Do you like to camp and hike? Do you enjoy being in the wild? Rafting gives you plenty of chances to do these things.

Finally, you should like excitement. If you do not, there are always Class I and Class II rivers for easy rafting. Real thrills are to be found in more advanced water.

If you like water, swimming, nature and excitement, then white-water rafting may be the sport for you.

Next, learn and understand more about the sport. How do rivers work? What features are needed in a raft? What are the best paddle strokes? These and many more questions can be answered by **white-water schools**. These schools give lessons on how to run rivers. Some schools plan trips and take you on rivers to learn techniques.

If you feel comfortable in the water, you may want to go on a river trip with family and friends. You do not need to own equipment to run a river. Many groups plan river trips. These groups, called outfitters, take care of all the details of a raft trip. All types of trips are available. You can have fancy food or snacks. You can camp or stay in hotels. The trips can last anywhere from a few hours to several weeks. It all depends on how much you want to do. For a list of outfitters, check your library.

River rafts and equipment are expensive. You should make sure you really like the sport before spending a lot of money. If you decide to buy your own equipment, always take good care of it. It can be your best friend on the river.

White-water fun is a sport you can enjoy for years. Why not get started now? Rivers all over the world are waiting for you.

Glossary

Bailing Bucket: A bucket used to remove water from the raft.

Canoe: A popular floating boat seen often on rivers. Once made from a hollow log.

Dogleg: A bend in the river.

Eddy: A place on the river where the water is calm or moves upstream.

Eskimo Roll: A technique used by kayakers to right themselves after turning upside down.

G-Rig: Craft developed by Georgie White by lashing three large rafts together.

Hypothermia: The condition of losing body heat. Can cause shivering, slowness, and sometimes death. One of the greatest dangers that boaters face.

Kayak: A long, thin, cigar-shaped craft.

Life Jacket: A vest that floats. Must be worn at all times while on the river.

Oarlock: The device that holds the oar onto the raft frame.

Outfitters: Groups that plan and hold river trips.

Paddle: Hand-held device that propels the boat. Consists of grip, shaft and blade.

Pontoons: Huge inflatable rafts used mainly on big rivers.

Rapids: Fast moving part of river. Waves and obstacles are present.

Reversal: A place where river currents meet in different directions. Can trap a boat. Also called souse holes, backrollers or keepers.

Shallows: Wide part of river that exposes many rocks.

Standing Wave: Also called haystacks. Waves caused from fast water striking slower water.

Strainers: Trees and other obstacles on a river.

Tongues: V-shaped chutes that enter rapids.

White Water: Water with obstacles.

White-Water School: Schools that teach how to run rivers.